© 2014 by E.C. Nakeli

Published by Perez Publishing LLC – *www.perezpublishing.com* –

For your questions and publishing needs write to:

Perez Publishing
548 Congressional Drive
Westminster, MD,
21158 USA
Email: *perezpublishing@gmail.com*

Printed in the United States of America

All rights reserved. No part of this publication may be reproduced, stored in a retrieval system, or transmitted in any form or by any means — for example, electronic, photocopy, recording — without the prior written permission of the publisher. The only exception is brief quotations in printed reviews.

E. C. Nakeli

To contact the author, write to:

E.C. Nakeli
Perez Publishing
548 Congressional Drive
Westminster, MD
21158 USA
Email:

ecnakeli@yahoo.com Living a

Life that Counts/E.C. Nakeli

ISBN: 978-0-9850668-7-1

Unless otherwise indicated, Scripture references are from
THE HOLY BIBLE, NEW INTERNATIONAL VERSION®, NIV®
Copyright © 1973, 1978, 1984, 2011 by Biblica, Inc.™

Used by permission. All rights reserved worldwide.

Living a Life that Counts:

How to Impact time and Eternity

Perez
Publishing
Breaking through... Breaking out

Table of Contents

Introduction……………………………………………………….1

Chapter 1: Background Exploits………………………..6

Chapter 2: Knowledge of God as One who hears……..14

Chapter 3: Righteousness………………….24

Chapter 4: Wholehearted Devotion to the Kingdom …29

Chapter 5: The Anointing of the Holy Spirit………..36

Chapter 6: Revelation Knowledge………………………….46

Chapter 7: The Leadership of the Holy Spirit………….53

Chapter 8: Expectations for Christ's Return……………62

Chapter 9: Faith in God's Promises……………………….79

Chapter 10: Knowledge of the God of the Promises…..88

In Conclusion:……………………………………………..112

Dedication

I dedicate this book to the late Rev Dr. Simon Epamba who has gone home to be with the Lord. He made his life counted for time and eternity by pouring everything into the service of the King and His people

Introduction

I was scheduled to minister in my friend Ps James Ekor-tah's church, with the main purpose of advertising my book, "When All Seems Fading". The normal thing for me to do, which I planned on doing, was to preach on a chapter from the book. As I waited on the Lord for His anointing and power in preparation for the ministry, I received a very strong impression that the Lord did not want me to share directly from the book. As I waited further on the Lord, He laid on my heart the message on "Living a Life That Counts" which I shared with the brethren that fateful Sunday. In fact the brethren where quite blessed because the message was coming not from me but from the Lord Himself. The all-knowing God knew the needs of the people and decided to meet the needs. About a year after I preached this message, I felt the Lord leading me to develop a book from it . How on earth would I develop a book from a single message? If it were a series of messages I would have understood, but because revelation comes from the Lord I decided to proceed to writing the book.

"Living a Life that Counts" is a very timely message from the Lord to His children in particular, and the world as whole. We live in a dispensation where people's lives are not counting for anything significant. People do things for the impression they can give and applause they can generate from men. People measure the importance of whatever is done in terms of the degree of human attention it can generate. My fear is that there seems to be a saturation of people willing to be of service as long as it puts them in the lime light and a dire shortage of those willing to do the things that will keep them in "obscurity". Whatever we do in this life must not be driven by the benefits of the now in terms of human applause, reward, or recognition. Our motivation must be the welfare of the King, the Kingdom, and its citizens. Ours must be hearts willing to please the King in everything we do.

This volume is going to be a little book designed to be read, possibly, in one sitting. We will be looking at the lives of two individuals in the Bible and from them drawing lessons which when applied will be of everlasting benefits to us . We do not want to waste our time in a life that ends when we draw our last breath in time. I believe like me, you have been looking for ways to make your life count in time and in eternity, reason why you have this book in your hands. My simple prayer for you is that my language will not only be clear to you, but that a spirit of urgency and a sustained motivation to continuously live a life that counts will be imparted to you by the Spirit of His glorious grace as you open your heart to His message for you this very hour.

May a holy detestation for the transient and ephemeral acclaims of all that is motivated by the desire for greatness and a sense of accomplishment as the world measures it be born in your heart as you go through the pages of this book. If after reading it your heart becomes sold out to nothing else but the glory of His Name, the expansion of

His Kingdom, the welfare of the citizens of the Kingdom, and the honor of the King, then I must have attained my goal for writing. You wouldn't want your life to count before men and count nothing before God.

The inspiration of this book will be drawn from the passage in Luke 2: 25-35; it's the story of Simeon, a very brief narrative of his later days. Though very brief, these verses can tell us a lot about the man and the impact of his life as measured by heaven. Follow me as we navigate through this brief study and learn little secrets we can all apply to live lives that count now and for eternity.

"Now there was a man in Jerusalem called Simeon, who was righteous and devout. He was waiting for the consolation of Israel, and the Holy Spirit was on him. [26] It had been revealed to him by the Holy Spirit that he would not die before he had seen the Lord's Messiah. [27] Moved by the Spirit, he went into the temple courts. When the parents brought in the child Jesus to do for him what the custom of the Law required, Simeon took him in his arms and praised God, saying:

> [29] "Sovereign Lord, as you have promised,
> you may now dismiss your servant in peace.
> [30] For my eyes have seen your salvation,
> [31] which you have prepared in the sight of all nations:
> [32] a light for revelation to the Gentiles,
> and the glory of your people Israel."

[33] The child's father and mother marveled at what was said about him. [34] Then Simeon blessed them and said to Mary, his mother: "This child is destined to cause the falling and rising of many in Israel, and to be a sign that will be spoken against, [35] so that the thoughts of many hearts will be revealed. And a sword will pierce your own soul too."

Chapter one

Background Exploits

The chronicles of Christian history have been written by ordinary men and women of little worth in the eyes of men but of great value in the eyes of God. Many a life unknown and hidden from the lime light of Christian fanfare is making tremendous impact in the spirit realm and moving the world God-ward. Some have chosen this lifestyle far removed from the podium of human recognition, celebration, and acclamation. Others have had no choice as a result of the circumstances life has put on them. Whatever the case there's one common virtue which characterizes these individuals: the desire to satisfy and please none other than the heart of the Father.

Our passage introduced Simeon thus: **"There was a man in Jerusalem called Simeon…"**

In this life it is not your title that matters before God but your exploits! It is not how you appear before men but who you are before God that counts. Simeon was just an obscure, unknown, unrecognized, and unappreciated ordinary man in Jerusalem, yet he was known and reckoned in heaven as a man of exploits.

He was not a priest or else the Bible would have told us so.

He was not a prophet or else the Bible would have told us so.

He was not a scribe or else the Bible would have told us so.

He was not a Pharisee or else the Bible would have told us so.

He was not a Sadducee or else the Bible would have told us too.

He was not a teacher of the Law or else the Bible would have told us so.

He was not even a Levite or else the Bible would have told us so too.

We live in a generation where men and women alike have a consuming passion for recognition and appellations. People are no longer contented being called by their names but by their man given titles. It seems to me that in the quest to be distinct from every other person, men are creating new titles everyday in order to distinguish themselves from those they consider ordinary. In some circles it's a rule to call all the titles when introducing an individual.

I was once in a meeting where the coordinator was about introducing the pastor of the house (let us assume his name was Jay), and she said something like, "let us welcome to the pulpit the man of the house Reverend, Prophet Jay, Doctor. She omitted the title "Doctor" after "Reverend", yet she sought to fit it in anywhere she could no matter how it sounded. I could see the look of fright in her face when she realized she left out one of the titles and so she quickly fitted it wherever there was room. Angels look at all this and are astonished at our increasing madness for titles. Some people would not respond when you call them unless you put all their titles in line and in order. Please do not misunderstand me; I have no problem with titles.

I personally believe that people should call you the way they feel comfortable. It is one thing when people, of their own volition call you by title(s), and a totally different thing when you demand to be called by a certain title such that others have to make sure they have all your titles in the correct order before addressing you. I was in one meeting when a minster was introduced as "His divine grace arch Bishop, Reverend, Doctor…" To say the least, I was flabbergasted and dismayed by the folly of the world that has taken such deep roots in the Kingdom, and the people of God seem to enjoy it.

Where are we heading to? What is becoming of the simplicity of the cross, and of the apostles and prophets? Have we been seduced to believe that the folly and hubris of the world is better than the self-effacing message and meekness of the cross? Increasingly, people are in search for the titles and appellations in such circles where people are judged and evaluated based on how many they have in front of their names, instead of the meekness and lowliness that comes from humble service to the people of God. Your commitment should be more to God than to the man-made councils that confer such titles upon whom they evaluate as competent with respect to their own set values.

The truth is I have met people with such titles who are meek and humble, and whose spirits dispense life because they are saturated with the anointing of the Holy Spirit. On the other hand I have met others with tittles, who are as dry as dry bones; you touch their spirits and no life comes out of it. Still I have met people; a few at most, without any such titles yet are men of spiritual power and authority, who dispense life as soon as you touch their spirits.

Listen to me my dear friend, a life that counts must be one of self-effacement and self-abasement. In the Kingdom there is no room for self-advertisement and self-aggrandizement. Anything done with the motive and intent to make you look better than anyone else counts for nothing! Your goal should be to achieve background exploits. Many people's goal is to belong to the religious order of this day. They want to be in the exclusive clubs of the "enlightened", even at the price of what the Lord God has called them to do in the private. They want to be celebrated even at the price of the truth, acclaimed even by hands and lips stained with the blood of the honest.

Like Simeon, if your life must count you must be someone totally given to doing only things that count before God, things that will stand the fire of judgment. You must become one who is acquainted with the presence of the King, known in the courts of heaven, recognized by the host of heaven, and respected by the hordes of hell.

Wherever you are, you can be doing things that people may never recognize you for. The truth is that you should know and be certain of the fact that the registry of heaven has whatever thing you do for God out of pure motives. And you will surely be rewarded for it. Nothing you do for God ever goes unnoticed if done out of pure motives, for the sole sake of expanding the Kingdom and the welfare of those in the King's domain.

It is sad that many people abandon what they are doing because man has failed to recognize them. It is mere human tendency to want to be recognized and appreciated for our actions. But we, the reborn, are not ordinary men and women. We have been transformed by the life from above and must allow that life to flow through us in whatever we find our hands doing.

Isn't it amazing to you that when God addresses people he does not use titles? He calls them by their names. Think about it, when John the Baptist was asked to tell who he was, he refused all the titles and described himself by his calling. I have met people with a list of titles who can't tell you their life goal. Their titles have made them more confused than they were without them. John told those who came to him, "I am the voice of one crying in the desert…" Yet we are told that he was a prophet in the order of Elijah, a harbinger to the King of glory in His earthly ministry. One whose birth, ministry, and death marked the transition between two dispensations in God's eternal calendar was known only as John the Baptizer. May we all set our hearts on the things that matter in the kingdom!

When I talk of background exploits what do I mean? I refer to those things you do which count only in the sight of the Lord God of heaven. I am referring to a life of consistent personal prayer, not about selfish requests, but prayer that seeks the advancement of His kingdom to the ends of the earth. I am talking of prayer whose paramount interest is the welfare of the Kingdom's citizens. When I talk of background exploits, I am referring to a life of personal praise and worship; a heart that sings to the Lord in joyful melody when no other human ears are listening; a life poured out in humble adoration to the eternal King of the universe. When I talk of background exploits I am talking of a life of behind the scenes-service to the saints; meeting the needs of God's people without drawing attention to yourself;

encouraging the downcast, praying with those who need prayer, teaching those who need to be taught and grounded in the word. I am talking of a life of personal fasting, Bible reading and study.

Chapter reflections

What are some things in your local church or neighborhood, which you can do without calling the attention and applause of men?

Can you create a prayer list of the pastors and leaders of your local church and pray for them even for ten minutes a week?

You can find someone whose needs you can meet, such that it is known only between you, the individual, and heaven that you met them.

You can make a list of the nations of the world and pray for each nation a day until you go through the list. These are just some of the background exploits you can carry out to make your life count for time and for eternity.

Chapter two
Knowledge of God as One who hears

His very name Simeon means, "The One who hears me." This tells us a great deal about the man whose life we are studying here. If your life must count in these last days you must be a man who hears heaven and whom heaven hears, and above all a man who believes he knows that heaven hears. Your life must be built on this simple fact that whatever you say heaven hears and records.

What will give you boldness and confidence in the time of emergency and adversity is knowledge of the fact that God hears you. It is the more reason why we must, as children of God place ourselves, permanently in a position to be heard of God. You must live in such a way that there is no barrier whatsoever in your communication line with the Throne room. Have you ever found yourself in an emergency situation in a place where even emergency calls cannot be made? You try and there is absolutely no signal to reach the person you have to? Well permit me say this is a small and faint comparison with the spiritual situation. Often you can tell when there is no cell phone signal and know for sure that your call can't go through. Spiritually it is easier to be self-deceived to think that you are actually connected meanwhile your cell line has even been disconnected. Sometimes we get out of spiritual network without even knowing it. I am not talking here of a physical location as some may misunderstand.

There is no physical location in this wide universe not covered by Heaven's Mobile Network. We have a coverage that spans the whole wide universe and extends beyond physical boundaries. And wherever you may find yourself every call is but a local call with unlimited airtime. Here i am referring to the spiritual condition and position in which a man may find himself, such that the communication lines become temporarily affected. If one knows that heaven would not hear him or if he is not sure whether or not heaven will hear him, his boldness and confidence in time of emergency is greatly affected.

If your life must count, you must know for sure that heaven hears;

1. **Your prayers**: once you place yourself in a position in which you are sure that heaven will hear you and respond to your prayers, then you must pray like you know it. And you must pray, believing and acting in a manner that shows you are certain heaven has heard. When you know that heaven has heard, you keep confessing and believing that you have received the answer no matter how long it may take for the response to be made manifest in the physical.

2. **Your cries**: Have you ever felt like crying? Have you ever wondered what heaven makes of your tears? I want to let you know that every tear you shed never goes in vain if it is shed for a just cause. Heaven hears your cries and records your tears. The Psalmist said, "Record my misery; list my tears on your scroll —

are they not in your record?" (Ps 56:8) Is it not amazing to know that God does not only hear your cries but that He records the tears produced by those cries? When is the last time you poured out your heart to God with cries? Have you bought the lies of the world which say only the weak cry? David's understanding of the power of tears made him a man who constantly poured out his aching heart to God. Sometimes cries bring healing. Of the Lord Jesus, the Bible says, " During the days of Jesus' life on earth, he offered up prayers and petitions with fervent cries and tears to the one who could save him from death, and he was heard because of his reverent submission." (He 5:7)

If crying is a symbol of weakness then I want to be a weak man in the order of David, Jeremiah, and the Lord Jesus. Pour out your heart with cries of intercession for a lost and sin-infested world. Pour out your heart in intercession for a Church that has lost the power of the Holy Spirit. Pour out your heart in fervent intercession for the strife, division, and competition that reigns amongst the people of God. Pour out your heart with cries for the saints who are living far below their inheritance in Christ. Even the silent cries of your heart are heard and recorded. Some people are too ashamed to cry outwardly yet their heart is full of tears. They want to appear strong before men yet cry in secret. Even those tears that fall from the eyes of your heart are seen and recorded by heaven. Talking of the Israelites in the midst of their suffering, God said to Moses, "I have heard them crying out..." Though it seemed as though for four hundred years and above He had not heard, He told Moses He had heard the cries of the children of Israel. I want to let you know that He has heard yours too.

3. **Your silent whispers**: Sometimes we are too weak to pray. Other times we are too weak to cry. All we

can do is whisper with the little strength we have left. At such moments it seems as though, our words though silent, are bouncing back to us. If you ever find yourself in such a situation, I am here to tell you even then heaven hears you. Remember when Hannah prayed in the temple? She spoke no audible words but her silent whispers touched the throne of grace and rent the heavens to create a doorway for her request to come to her

Now you must understand that just as heaven hears and records your prayers, cries and whispers so it does your complaints, murmurings, grumbling, criticisms, gossips, and slander. Every word that comes out of your mouth is taken seriously by heaven. Those spoken in public and those spoken in the closet. God takes seriously whatever you say. In the book of Numbers 14:28, the Lord says, "So tell them, 'As surely as I live, declares the LORD, I will do to you the very thing I heard you say". In order words you are the architect of your own destiny. The words you speak are tracers that influence the path your life will take. They are materials you provide for the building of your future. Your words are the pillars which will hold the edifice of your destiny. They are the fence around the garden of your life. They are seeds to sow in the garden of your life. They are the most potent weapons you can use for your victory or defeat. If you don't like the outcome, then don't say it. God will do to you according to what He has heard you say. That is why it is so important to fill your heart with the word of God so that out of its abundance the mouth will speak. So, instead of grumbling and complaining, offer thanks and praises! Instead of criticizing pray constructively. In this way, you will be making your life to count for time and for eternity.

Chapter reflection

Hearing God is an important aspect of the Christian life which many neglect. If you have to make a difference, you must develop the habit of hearing God. When is the last time you asked the Lord to speak to you?

Create time within the next week to just go into God's presence to listen.

As you read the word of God, write down things you feel the Lord is telling you from His word and step out to obey.

God speaks to us in diverse ways, try to list down some ways you think God uses to speak to you and see how you can develop that area.

Chapter Three
Righteousness

Righteousness talks of being in a right standing with God. Your right standing with God is twofold: firstly it comes from the imputed righteousness of Christ Jesus to you by His death on the cross on your behalf. Because Jesus died, you can have a right standing with God by accepting His finished work on the cross of Calvary. If you have confessed Jesus and made Him your Lord and Savior, then He has become for you your righteousness from God (see 1Co 1:31). When God looks at you, in a sense, He sees you clothed in His own very righteousness. Therefore He sees His own nature and attribute in you and on you. The Bible says, "But now apart from the law the righteousness of God has been made known, to which the Law and the Prophets testify. [22] This righteousness is given through faith in Jesus Christ to all who believe. There is no difference between Jew and Gentile" (Ro 3:21-22a).

The righteousness of God is a gift that has been given to you because of your confession and faith in Christ Jesus. This is what gives you the right standing before the Father. Now that God has clothed you in His righteousness because of your confession of Christ Jesus, you ought to live and walk in this righteousness by aligning your life and actions to what God has done for you and in you. This is the second side of righteousness. Many people think that all that matters is the imputed righteousness. If it were so then anyone who has made a confession of Christ but is living in deliberate sin will still be allowed in heaven. Your acts of righteousness, your words of righteousness, and your thoughts in righteousness are what seal the righteousness of God imputed to you as a result of the death of Christ thereby making you a candidate for heaven.

Of Simeon, the Bible says he was a righteous man. In other words his thoughts, words, and actions were in line with the Word of God. And that is how God expects you and me to live today. Our whole life must be in accordance with the word; our choices, values, principles, motives and intents, inclinations and the like must agree with, and be based on the word of God. The Bible talks of us working out our salvation with fear and trembling. That is, God's righteousness in us and on us must be revealed in our thoughts, words, and actions. If your life must count for time and for eternity, you must walk in righteousness.

Throughout history, those who have walked in righteousness have made their lives to count before the God of heaven and His angels. These have been men respected by hell and esteemed by heaven. Job's life counted in his day because of his righteousness. Noah's life counted in his day and beyond because of his righteousness. Your life will make a difference if you live and walk in righteousness. The Bible says righteousness exalts. You want to be exalted by God above your competitors? Let righteousness become your watch word. As corrupt as the world may be, the natural man wants to deal with people who deal righteously. You can make your life to count before the One who matters. He is the One who has the last word. At the end all the opinions and political correctness of men will not count. You can make your life to count by living righteously.

Chapter reflection

Are there some things in your thought life, language or action that do not agree with the word of God?

What steps can you take to get rid of them or bring them in agreement with the word of God?

Make a checklist of such things and beside them right down ways you will get rid of them. Set a goal for yourself and pray for the enabling of the Holy Spirit.

Chapter Four

Wholehearted Devotion to the Kingdom

People who impact the world for God are men and women whose hearts are fully committed and devoted to the Lord. Do you want to impact your world for God? Do you want your life to count for time and for eternity? Do you want to make a lasting difference in lives that will outlive you? Then devote your heart totally to the Lord and the cause of the Kingdom. The Bible says Simeon was devout. This means he was serious, sincere, and performed his duties as a child of God with total commitment.

Throughout the pages of the Book, you find that those who made a difference in their generation and whose lives and impact counted in their lifetime and beyond are those who served God wholeheartedly; completely devoted to Kingdom'scourse. God demands of you and me nothing short of a wholehearted commitment on our part in whatever sphere or domain we are called to serve in. So that this does not sound high and impractical, let me take you through some very simple and definite ways you may want to qualify wholeheartedness to the Kingdom:

Passionate Worship:

Your worship of God must be with passion if your devotion is wholehearted. Worship and praise from your heart and lips should be spontaneous as evidence of a heart that is totally committed to the Kingdom. The Lord described David as a man after God's own heart primarily because of his passionate worship that expressed his desire for God, the house of God, and the things of God. From the depth of his heart David cried out, "As the deer pants for streams of water, so my soul pants for you, my God. My soul thirsts for God, for the living God. When can I go and meet with God?" (Ps 42:1-2) A heart that yearns, longs, and calls after God is a heart filled with passionate worship for the King of creation. May your heart be filled with passion for the living God!

Faithful Service:

Another simple yet effective measurement or manifestation of wholehearted devotion to the Kingdom is faithfulness in service. Faithful service is one that is done not because of the recognition or appreciation that comes from man but service done as unto the Lord. In such a case whether man acknowledges your service or not you keep up with it because your focus is your God. The apostle Paul wrote. "Serve wholeheartedly, as if you were serving the Lord, not people" (Eph 6:7). In wholehearted service the focus of the servant is God. You offer your service as though it was done directly to God.

When Jehoshaphat was carrying out reforms in the land of Israel, he told the officials he appointed "You must serve faithfully and wholeheartedly in the fear of the LORD". Faithfulness and wholeheartedness in service to the Lord and His people cannot be separated. You cannot be unfaithful in your service of Him and claim to be wholeheartedly devoted to His course. Another ingredient of wholehearted service to the Lord is to serve Him with a willing mind. Your degree of willingness in the things of the kingdom shows the degree to which you are wholeheartedly devoted to Him. David told his son Solomon. "And you, my son Solomon, acknowledge the God of your father, and serve him with wholehearted devotion and with a willing mind, for the LORD searches every heart and understands every desire and every thought." (1Ch 28:9) How willing are you to be used by God? If your life must count in this life and the one to come, you must be passionate in worship and faithful in service as Simeon was.

Consistent Obedience:

Obedience to the word and voice of God to do things both great and small in a consistent manner will make your life count in this side of eternity and beyond. Sometimes what it takes to make a difference is rendering obedience in things that appear foolish and unreasonable in the sight of man. When we disobey God in some things, we sometimes ground whatever obedience we were building on. We must continue on the path of obedience if our lives must count for time and beyond. The Bible says, "LORD, the God of Israel, there is no God like you in heaven or on earth—you who keep your covenant of love with your servants who continue wholeheartedly in your way." (2Ch 6:14) The key word there is "continue". This means those who consistently obey the Lord, His covenant of love will be their portion. If your life must count you must renounce, reject, and rebuke any area of disobedience in your life. Refuse to have an affair with the demon called disobedience; it seeks but to render you ineffective and inefficient in your service to the Lord.

Wholesome Love:

Why do I use the adjective "wholesome" to qualify love? The main reason is because the term has been hackneyed and rarely connotes its true meaning when used. Many have mistaken love for indulgence and compromise. When they say, "You don't love me" they mean "you have refused to compromise with me and indulge my sin." Wholesome love tells the truth, corrects, rebukes, and disciplines when need be. It does not seek to exploit others and use them for one's own advantage. It is wholesomeness in your love for the people of God and for humanity which will cause you to give up your comfort and privacy to make room for another. It is wholesome love that gives birth to compassion in your heart for the sick and the suffering. It is the birthplace of sacrifice, self-abasement, and self-effacement.

A life motivated by love is the life that counts beyond the confine of self and pettiness of clicks and factions. It sees beyond the differences that have plagued humankind to our common need for love and grace. Wholesome love breaks the barriers of racial, tribal, social, and religious class to extend a hand to whomever needs it. You can make your life to count more than you can imagine by demonstrating the love of God and His Christ where He has put you, using the resources He has blessed you with.

Chapter reflection

Are you aware of anything in your heart that makes your devotion to the Lord divided? Now by an act of faith, get rid of it and offer your heart totally to God.

After getting rid of the things you know are causing your heart to be divided, you can now ask the Lord to show you the things you are not aware of.

Now ask the Lord to take total control of your heart. Consciously offer Him your heart and ask Him to keep it for you.

Chapter Five
The Anointing of the Holy Spirit

To make a difference that counts in whatever you do in this life, more so for it to count beyond this life, you need the anointing of the Holy Spirit in your life. The world is tired of the gimmicks and gymnastics that originate from itself and is looking for something that is different. What can offer this world anything different is what is done by the anointing of the Holy Spirit. The problem is that increasingly even children of the Most High fail to understand the purpose of the anointing and therefore fail to tap its extraordinary and supernatural resources. It doesn't matter your sphere or domain of service, what you need is the anointing of the Holy Spirit in order to function at a level that will put you above your peers and competitors. It is the anointing upon your life that will make you different and give you an edge over those who do not have a right to the Spirit's anointing.

Of Simeon, the Bible says, "The Holy Spirit was upon him…" It is the anointing upon his life that made his life to count and find a place in the account of the Bible. Though he seems to have spent his days in obscurity, he was in the lime light of heaven. Angels reckoned him as a man of consequence. He was known in hell as a man with the seal of the Holy Spirit upon his life. I do not know how to say it with a greater emphasis; what will take you beyond the sphere of human training and knowledge is the anointing of the Spirit on whatever you do. What the world needs today is not more education or more training or whatever humans can offer but the difference that can be made only by those with the anointing upon their lives.

As a believer, you have the right to two kinds of anointing; the anointing within and the anointing upon.

The Anointing Within

When you made a commitment to the Lord Jesus Christ with sincerity of heart, He came to live in you in the person of the Holy Spirit. There was a deposit of Himself in you by the Holy Spirit. It is this anointing of the Holy Spirit in you that identifies you as a child of God and gives you the right to your inheritance in Christ Jesus. Every believer has this anointing within him or her. The apostle John wrote, "As for you, the anointing you received from him remains in you…" (1Jn 2:27a)

As we yield in obedience and faith to the Lord the deposit in us may increase and then we become filled with the Holy Spirit. The sad thing is that many never go past this point of the initial deposit to the level of being filled with the Holy Spirit. The will of God for you is that you be filled with the Holy Spirit. You must seek to increase the level of your anointing within.

The Anointing Upon

There is also the anointing upon which comes to us to enable us do the extraordinary. As we said of Simeon, the bible says the Holy Spirit was upon him. The Lord Jesus said, "The Spirit of the Lord is upon me…" It is the anointing upon the believer that enables him to function with ease and efficiency. If the Son of God needed the anointing upon, then you and I need it most.

The truth is that whether it is the anointing within, or the anointing upon, you need it to make the difference in whatever you do. It is for every believer no matterthe sphere of your calling. You need the anointing to excel in your academics if you are a student. Even if you are an A-student without the anointing, you could be a genius with the anointing. You need the anointing in your business if you are a business man. You need the anointing to excel in your job whatever it may be. You need the anointing to build and keep meaningful relationships. Above all you need the anointing to function in your ministry. The anointing is not for preachers and ministers only, it's for every Spirit-born, blood-washed child of God.

The seal of the anointing on our lives is what gives authenticity, before God, to whatever we do. Without the seal of the anointing what we do will not count both in time and in eternity! It is indispensable for you to seek to be filled with the Holy Spirit and to have His anointing upon your life.

What the anointing will do for you

It will set you apart from the crowd: Many of us live our lives lost in the crowd of confusion, purposelessness, and mediocrity. When Jesus was in the midst of the crowd by the Jordan River, it was the anointing on Him that distinguished Him from anyone else. John said, "And I myself did not know him, but the one who sent me to baptize with water told me, 'The man on whom you see the Spirit come down and remain is the one who will baptize with the Holy Spirit.' (Jn 1:33) The Spirit of the Lord upon you will cause those who matter to the fulfilling of your destiny to recognize you. Do not go about seeking the recognition of men. Seek the anointing of the Holy Spirit and that anointing will bring recognition from those who matter.

It will set you high above your peers: what transformed Joseph from a prisoner to a prince was the anointing of God in his life. When he interpreted the dreams of pharaoh and gave direction on what had to be done to save the country, this is what Pharaoh said, "Can we find anyone like this man, one in whom is the spirit of God?" When the court of pharaoh recognized the Spirit within Joseph, he took the bold step to crown him second in command. My sisters and brothers, the world is looking for a difference, and what brings that difference is the anointing of the Holy Spirit.

It will terrorize your enemies: there are believers who are afraid of the enemy and of their enemies. Isaiah said, "And they shall fear the name of Jehovah from the west, and from the rising of the sun, his glory. When the adversary shall come in like a flood, the Spirit of Jehovah will lift up a banner against him." (Isa 59:9, Darby) It is the Spirit of the Lord upon you that will put the enemy to flight. That is why some people are a no-go zone for Satan and his cohorts. They steer clear of them and their affairs because the Spirit of the Lord on such terrorizes the enemy. An alternate translation of that verse reads, "The Spirit of the Lord will put him to flight". Do you want the enemy put to flight at your approach? Seek the anointing of the Holy Spirit.

It will make you a warrior: the anointing of God on your life will make you a warrior. It will transform you from a fearful weakling to a bold and courageous warrior for God. "The **Spirit** of the LORD came on him, so that he became Israel's judge and went to war. The LORD gave Cushan-Rishathaim king of Aram into the hands of Othniel, who overpowered him." (Jgs 3:10)
"Then the **Spirit** of the LORD came on Gideon, and he blew a trumpet, summoning the Abiezrites to follow him." (Jgs 6:34)

It will stir you out of complacency: there are moments when you feel complacent, indulgent, and want to stay on the plain of mediocrity and compromise. It is the anointing of the Holy Spirit on you that stirs you at such moments to begin or to keep pursuing your destiny. You never need to coax or cajole a man who has the anointing upon his life; the Spirit of God will do it. Of Samson, the

Bible says, "and the Spirit of the LORD began to stir him while he was in Mahaneh Dan, between Zorah and Eshtaol."(Jgs 13:25) There are so many people caught in the middle of one thing or another knowing not what direction to take. They find themselves between and betwixt, caught in the middle of their own Zorah and Eshtaol. When the Spirit of the Lord comes upon you, you will be stirred up and set on the path to fulfilling your destiny.

Because this is not a book on the Holy Spirit, I will beg to end here for now. We will deal with this in detail in our book, "When the Holy Spirit Comes".

Chapter Reflection

How desperate are you to walk in the anointing of the Holy Spirit?

How willing are you to be led by Him even in the mundane things of your daily life.

You see, your productivity and efficiency depend on your relationship with the Holy Spirit. The validity and acceptability of what you do in the Kingdom depends on whether it has the seal of the Spirit on it.

Chapter six
Revelation knowledge

Revelation knowledge is the bedrock for distinction and extraordinary accomplishments. It is what draws the line between the strong and the weak, victims and victors, winners and losers, great and small. The amount of revelation knowledge is what gives you an edge over others who do not possess such knowledge. Speak to the great and they will tell you that it is something they discovered or better still which was revealed to them, that others did not know, and that set them apart.

The truth is that you can only truly serve God to the degree of revelation you have received. When you serve God based only on the revelation of others, service will soon become a boredom and drudgery. What information do I have that others need but do not have? How can I make this information available to them? People are looking for those who will make a difference in their lives. That is why the apostle Paul prayed thus for the church in Ephesus: "I keep asking that the God of our Lord Jesus Christ, the glorious Father, may give you the Spirit of wisdom and revelation, so that you may know him better. [18] I pray that the eyes of your heart may be enlightened in order that you may know the hope to which he has called you, the riches of his glorious inheritance in his holy people, [19] and his incomparably great power for us who believe" (Eph 1:17-19)

From the above passage we see that the spirit of revelation goes hand in glove with the spirit of wisdom. Revelation knowledge is what will cause you to know God better. Revelation knowledge is what will fill you with expectation, and expectation is the gateway to great accomplishments. Revelation knowledge will lead you to appropriate that which is your inheritance in Christ Jesus, and to experience the great power of the Holy Spirit available to us who call His Name. You need revelation knowledge before you can begin to comprehend the God you serve, what He has done for you, what He has done in you, what He has made of you, and what He can do through you.

About Simeon, the Bible says, "It had been revealed to him by the Holy Spirit that…" He was a man whose life was marked by revelation. God wants to bring us to such a place, where our lives are marked by personal revelation of Himself and of events and things which matter. For your life to count, you need revelation knowledge.

Why revelation knowledge?

What caused Joseph to rise to the throne of second in command of Egypt? It was the revelation knowledge from the spirit of wisdom that rested upon him. By revelation he spoke words of wisdom that altered the course of the history of humankind and therefore made a difference which counted beyond his day. What about Joseph the husband of Mary? It was revelation knowledge that caused him to not divorce Mary and therefore expose her to public disgrace and eventual death by stoning. Of course needless to say, without such revelation to Joseph, God's plan of redemption for the human race would have been abortive. It was revelation knowledge to him that preserved the life of the baby-King from the plans of Herod.

The truth is that there are so many things we lose to the attacks from hell because of lack of revelation knowledge. Revelation knowledge will preserve you in the days of adversity, sustain you in times of weakness, and free you from bondage to traditions of men and religious systems. What about Jacob? All along he had slaved for his uncle Laban, but had little to show for all his time of hard work and toilsome labor. The turning point in his life was marked when the angel of the Lord spoke to him in his dream. A secret was revealed to him which changed his life from a poor man to one who had more than enough. He became exceedingly wealthy because of revelation. What hard work did not accomplish for over twenty years, revelation knowledge accomplished in the split of a second. O God, fill us with revelation knowledge. Stir our hearts and set us on the path to pursue a life marked by revelation. May it be said of you, at least by heaven's court that "it had been revealed to him that…"

When you receive revelation about a thing, it is easier to stake your life for it. What do you think caused reformers like Martin Luther to risk their lives for the truth? It is because they received revelation knowledge of what the truth is. And their revelation knowledge has made their lives to count for centuries and will continue to count till eternity. Great scientist and mathematicians like Newton, Pascal, Faraday and many others tell us they owe their discoveries to revelation knowledge. The revelation knowledge of Daniel set him apart for greatness in a foreign land as an exile in captivity.

By the Spirit of revelation upon my life I speak to you to receive the spirit of revelation in the name of Jesus. I tear every veil of blindness from the eyes of your heart and command you to see the un-seeable., to perceive the intangible, and to know the unknowable. Some people are afraid to ask for revelation; I am here to tell you that you need not be afraid. The apostle Paul asked for it for the whole church in Ephesus. In fact the Lord himself invites us to ask, seek, and knock on the door of revelation. In the book of Jeremiah He says, "Call to me and I will answer you and tell you great and unsearchable things you do not know." (Je 33:3) This tells us that God is more willing to dispense of revelation than we are willing and let alone ready to receive. Great and unsearchable things are things that will fascinate the most astute human mind. They are things that will not be discovered by a million years of research and study.

If your life is filled with the Holy Spirit, it will be marked by revelation knowledge because the Spirit of God is the revealer of the mysteries of God. He is the one who reveals; man cannot reveal anything to you. I may come with the most wonderful revelation and speak a million words but if the Spirit of God does not illuminate what I say in your mind, it will amount to nothing. Revelation is what transforms head knowledge to heart and life experience.

The Bible talks of those who are always learning but never coming to the knowledge of the truth. This is due to the lack of revelation knowledge. The truth can only be grasped and apprehended by revelation. People can know fact in the head but the truth can only be known in the heart. That is why it is easy, very easy to detect truth from lies when you listen with the ears of your heart. I have made up my mind to always listen to people with the ears of my heart. It makes a whole deal of difference. When you listen with your heart you can even hear the unspoken words in the heart of menbecause your heart connects to the person's heart. There are times when I am able to tell someone what he or she is thinking. Everyday I pray for the spirit of revelation. No matter the level of revelation I may be receiving now, there is still room to improve and be able to hear God better and see beyond the normal. Make it your habit to ask God not just for revelation but for the spirit of revelation if your life must count in time and in eternity.

Chapter Reflection

What is your primary source of information? How often do you take time to listen to the Holy Spirit for revelation knowledge? How much time do you spend soaked in the Word for a release of the Rhema into your spirit? Have you ever asked God for the Spirit of revelation? Revelation knowledge draws the line between people or equal potentials and uplifts those who possess it far above the highest level they could ever attain. One revelation and you are decades ahead of everyone else who lacks it.

Chapter seven

The Leadership of the Holy Spirit

In this world today many people are led by many different things; some are led by their worldly wisdom, others by their traditions, others by their strong will, some by their likes and dislikes, and others by the opinions of men. If your life must count these last days and for eternity, you must be moved and led by nothing but the Holy Spirit. As believers, our lives must as a whole be led by the Spirit of the living God. We are not to live our lives compartmentally, letting the Holy Spirit lead us in some aspects and leading ourselves the way we want in the other aspects of life. Some people depend on the Holy Spirit when it comes to their spiritual life but leave Him out when it comes to their finances and daily choices. In a generation where too many things are calling for the believer's attention, where there are several opportunities knocking at the door of the believer and calling for his or commitment, it takes the voice of the

Holy Spirit to be able to make the right choices and resist the wrong voices calling out loudly and persistently.

The Bible says of Simeon, "...Led by the Holy Spirit..." God is building a generation of men and women who will be led by nothing but by His Spirit; men and women, boys and girls who are spiritual enough not to trust their own thinking and judgments. How do you know that this awesome opportunity is not the will of God for you except the Spirit leads you to choose rightly? I have been thrilled to discover that the Lord is interested in guiding and leading us even in the minutest details of our lives. That is why He has promised that, "I will instruct you and teach you in the way you should go, I will counsel you with my loving eye on you." (Ps 32:8) It is your responsibility to claim this divine promise for yourself daily. It will make all the difference whether or not you will be led daily by the Spirit of God. In fact the leadership of the Holy Spirit is what characterizes you as a child of God. He says in His word that,

"For those who are led by the Spirit of God are the children of God" (Ro 8:14).

In a sense, every child of God is led by the Spirit of God to different degrees. In that same chapter of the book of Romans, in verse nine, Paul wrote, "You, however, are not in the realm of the flesh but are in the realm of the Spirit, if indeed the Spirit of God lives in you. And if anyone does not have the Spirit of Christ, he does not belong to Christ." If you are a child of God, then you have the anointing within you. If you have the anointing within you, then that anointing teaches you and guides you though sometimes you may be unaware of it. Read that verse again and you will find the deepest of truths revealed by Paul therein. Paul says you and I are living in the realm of the Spirit. If we remain in His realm all the time, His leadership in our daily affairs will become something so second- nature to us. The problem with us most often is that we leave the realm of the Spirit into that of the flesh and natural thinking. It is possible to stay in the realm of the Spirit and from there carry out the daily routines of our lives. When you are in that realm, you have access to information that others do not have and this gives you a supernatural edge.

Now, the question is "how can you improve on your Spirit led life?" I will seek to answer this question in the next paragraphs.

Living in the realm of the Spirit

For your life to count in time and eternity, you must live in the realm of the Spirit of God. You are only as strong as you are led by Him. And you are led by Him as you live in His realm. Here are a few ways you can improve on your capacity to be led by the Spirit of God.

- Know His voice: The voice of the Spirit is the voice of Jesus. Jesus said His sheep know His voice and follow it. You and I must become acquainted with the voice of the Holy Spirit so that we can be effectively led by Him. If we don't get to know His voice then though He may speak and call, we may unconsciously miss it or ignore it. In this domain we all need to be trained by Him and by those who have learned through experience to identify His voice. As you keep hearing His voice and become acquainted to it, you will realize that with time it becomes easier to hear Him speak than it was at the beginning.

- Be willing to be led: If you are to live in the realm of the Spirit, you must be willing to be led by Him. Being willing simply means keeping a position of surrender to the will of God. It means expecting His leadership in whatever you do, looking forward in anticipation to what He will say next or where He will lead next. It is this anticipation of His leadership that keeps you in His realm. I have discovered that when I live in expectation and anticipation of the move of the Spirit, I more readily move in His realm. And this accounts for every difference that has been made in my life.

- Confess your need: Another way to improve on your ability to be led by the Holy Spirit is to confess you need for His leadership. When you show the Spirit that you need Him to lead and guide you in whatever you do, it gives Him the permission to speak to you. Ask the Lord to guide you daily when you get up. As you progress in the activities of the day continuously ask His guidance and leadership. Pause often to listen to His voice. Ask for sensitivity to His voice and for malleability in His hands.

- Be ready to be led: To be led by the Spirit, to live in His realm, you must be ready to be led by Him. Readiness talks of ensuring that there is nothing in your life which can obstruct or silence His voice. You must be ready to lay aside your own preconceived ideas and dispositions. Readiness talks of the capacity to embrace His will even when you do not understand the intricacies of it. The areas in my life which have been void of the Spirit's leadership are those areas where I have had my own preconceived notions, ideas, qualities etc. But when

I have brought myself to a neutral gear, so to speak, guidance and leadership have been a lot easier.

- Depend on His faithfulness: Because we cannot even trust our own judgments, sometimes you think you are in neutral disposition meanwhile your heart is already inclined to one particular direction. Sometimes there may be things, unknown to you, which may hinder you from hearing His voice. In such situations all you can do is to trust His mercies and His faithfulness. He has promised to lead and guide you and His word is forever true. Though we should do our best to be willing, ready, and expect His leadership, we should and must never rely on our human capacities for any of these things. His faithfulness alone is what you should depend on.

- Thank Him Often for His guidance: The latitude and magnitude of anything you receive will depend on your attitude to gratitude; a grateful heart makes room for more. As you thank the Lord for His faithfulness in guiding and leading you, His guidance and leadership will increase greatly. As you progress into your day, thank Him for the guidance He has provided you already, those you are conscious of and those you may never be aware of till the other side of time.

As you seek to be led by Him you will be making your life to count.

Chapter Reflection

How often do you yield to the inner voice of the Spirit within you? What about yielding to His promptings and nudges? How malleable are you in the hands of the Holy Spirit? Until we learn to completely yield to Him we forfeit entering into the fullness of our inheritance. It is His leadership that qualifies you as a mature son who is ready to receive his inheritance.

Chapter Eight
Expectation of Christ's Return

If there is one thing that will keep you focused and make your life to count, it is the degree of your expectation for the return of Christ the King in a short while. The difference between the way men and women live their lives is based on how far they have grasped the truth of the return of eternity's King and bridegroom. Like in the days of Noah and Lot, many people fail to heed the call to find shelter from the coming destruction of this present world and its system. Increasingly it seems many more people are getting entangled in the web of worldly cares and things which do not matter beyond the nearest future. Those whose lives are counting now and will count for eternity are those filled with expectation for the return of the King of the universe.

Of Simeon, the Bible says he was waiting for the consolation of Israel, which was the birth of the Messiah, that is, the first coming of the Lord. It was his preoccupation and earnest prayer, looking forth to the day that the Messiah would be born. For those of us living in this dispensation, we are no longer waiting for the consolation of Israel but for the consolation of the Church, the return of her Bridegroom. Since you are part of the Church you are a part of the Bride of Christ. Does it not bring pain to your heart that the Bridegroom has taken so long to come? Are you not bleeding with an ardent desire to see Him revealed to this generation in His glory and splendor? Whether you live your life with a sense of urgency or in complacency and indulgence greatly depends on whether or not you are living in expectation for His return.

There are many who profess His Name who do not believe that Jesus is coming soon and so have no expectation for His return. I was talking with some brethren about how the times are drawing to their close as all the signs are pointing. To my greatest shock, a young man asked in total disappointment, "why would Jesus want to come but in my own day?" In other words he was saying he has not yet accomplished what he has to accomplish in life so Jesus should not come and disrupt his program. He was honest enough to expose the condition of his lost heart by the question he asked; but there are many who may be singing songs and making statements that make them appear eager for His return yet their inward desire is for Him to come in the most distant future.

Let me ask you some questions that will set you thinking; are you living in expectation for the return of the King? Whatare you doing to hasten His return? Do your desires align with those things which will ensure that the King returns and returns quickly? There is no bride who does not long for the return of the bridegroom when he is away unless there is something deeply and fundamentally wrong in their relationship. May be the fact that you care nothing whether he returns soon or not is a betrayal of the fact that there is something fundamentally and deeply wrong in your relationship with Him.

Listen, and let me shock you; a shock that will revolutionize your life. It doesn't matter what you profess, you are not ready for His coming and will not go with Him when He comes if you are not living in expectation for the return of the King. With the testimony of two or three witnesses a matter is established. And I want to establish this matter with you:

"Now there is in store for me the crown of righteousness, which the Lord, the righteous Judge, will award to me on that day—and not only to me, but also to all who have longed for his appearing." (2Ti 4:8) The Lord Jesus is coming with His reward, and the reward is for those who have longed and are longing for His appearing. Again, let me ask you, are you longing for His appearing?

"So Christ was sacrificed once to take away the sins of many; and he will appear a second time, not to bear sin, but to bring salvation to those who are waiting for him." (He 9:28) This is my second witness; Christ is bringing His salvation to those who are waiting for Him. Are you expecting the return of the King?

Heed the admonishment

The apostle Paul admonished his mentee, pastor of the Church in Ephesus in the following words: "In the presence of God and of Christ Jesus, who will judge the living and the dead, ***and in view of his appearing and his kingdom***, I give you this charge: ² Preach the word; be prepared in season and out of season; correct, rebuke and encourage—with great patience and careful instruction. ³ For the time will come when people will not put up with sound doctrine. Instead, to suit their own desires, they will gather around them a great number of teachers to say what their itching ears want to hear. ⁴ They will turn their ears away from the truth and turn aside to myths. ⁵ But you, keep your head in all situations, endure hardship, do the work of an evangelist, discharge all the duties of your ministry." (1Ti 4:1-5, emphasis added)

Paul was telling Timothy that his whole live should be built "in view of His appearing". He asked him to make his live count by

- Preaching the word: many people are preaching but they are not preaching the word. They tell their stories and entertain the congregation and totally keep aside the word. If your life must count in these last days you must preach the word. Share the word at home, with your neighbors, with your colleagues, at every opportunity. In many a pulpit preachers spend their time preaching their man-made doctrines. Even ordinary church members who go out for evangelism fail to preach the word. They go out to spread their doctrines instead of the word of God.
- Be prepared in season and out of season: Paul asked Timothy to be loaded and ready to discharge at all times in order to make his life count in view of the appearing of the King. Like a soldier you must be ready at any one time to fight the battle into which you have engaged. Be ready to respond to the call and command of your Commander in Chief each time He sounds the trumpet. Be prepared to be taken

away if he should appear this second. Live prepared and ready.

- Keep your head in all situations (stay in control): In this life there are many things which will try to make you lose your head. Some things just come to get you off focus into confusion. Paul says for your life to count in view of His coming you must ensure that nothing makes you to lose control of yourself and your purpose and drive in life. You must always stay in control if your life must count. Keep your head in all situations!

- Endure hardship: enduring hardship is one sure way to make your life count for time and for eternity. Many people never go past a certain stage in life because they easily give up and give in in the face of hardship. Hardships are natural occurrences to separate the ranks of those who are willing to pay the price and those who are out for adventure. Resolve in your heart that you will endure hardship and that nothing will prevent you from reaching out with all you are and have towards the prize God has set for you.

- Do the work of an evangelist: the urgency of the time requires you and me to bring in the harvest. Let us use every opportunity to do the work of an evangelist. By so doing we will be making our lives to count for time and for eternity.

- Discharge all the duties of your ministry: by asking Timothy to discharge all the duties of his ministry, Paul was asking him to do all that he had the means and the ability to do for the expansion of the Kingdom of God. If your life must count for time and for eternity, you must use all your resources to promote and expand the kingdom of God. You must use your talents and abilities for the expansion of the kingdom. That is what will make your life count both in time and eternity.

Results for expecting His return

Why is it so important for you to live in expectation for the return of the King? Are there any other benefits associated with expecting His return? Let us look at some of them:

"Since everything will be destroyed in this way, what kind of people ought you to be? You ought to live holy and godly lives [12] as you look forward to the day of God and speed its coming.[a] That day will bring about the destruction of the heavens by fire, and the elements will melt in the heat. [13] But in keeping with his promise we are looking forward to a new heaven and a new earth, where righteousness dwells.

[14] So then, dear friends, since you are looking forward to this, make every effort to be found spotless, blameless and at peace with him." (2Pe 3:11-14)

"What I mean, brothers and sisters, is that the time is short. From now on those who have wives should live as if they do not; ³⁰ those who mourn, as if they did not; those who are happy, as if they were not; those who buy something, as if it were not theirs to keep;" (1Co 7:29-31)

"Dear friends, now we are children of God, and what we will be has not yet been made known. But we know that when Christ appears,[a] we shall be like him, for we shall see him as he is. ³ All who have this hope in him purify themselves, just as he is pure." (1Jn 3:12-3)

It will determine your platform

By platform, I mean the principles and values on which you build your life, the position you will take in different aspects of life. Those who are living in expectation of the return of the Lord Jesus Christ build their lives on the principles of God's word. If your life must count, it must be built on the word of God and not the opinion of the world. Many people are founding their lives on the faulty foundations of the philosophy of this world. No doubt such lives crumble in the test of adversity.

It will determine your perspective

Your perspective is simply the angle from which you view things or people. When you live with the expectation for the return of the Master, you see things and people from a whole new perspective, in light of eternity. You ask yourself when you meet anybody, "where is this one heading to?" and once you answer the question, you labor to see how that one can be helped to better prepare for eternity. When you have the opportunity to use things, you ensure that such things will better help you and others prepare for eternity. Of course you know that a person's perspective depends on where he is standing and the direction he is facing. That is why we talked first of the platform. If you stand on the platform of His word and view things through the eyes of eternity, you will make every second of your life to count. Because Simeon had eternity in view he was able to recognize the Messiah when the religious leaders of his time were preoccupied with their religious values. He saw with eternity's eyes. Oh! What perspective to view things from!

It will determine your priorities

You can know what counts in a man's life by the priorities he gives to such things. There are some things which do not count the least to some people because of the platform they are on and the perspective through which things are viewed. What are the things which have precedence in your finances, relationships, time, energy, and other resources? What value do you give to different things and what determines that value? What is your scale of preference, and what things appear at the top? For your life to count for time and eternity you must have the right priorities; and these must be things that matter in the sight of the Lord; kingdom things that expand the Kingdom in one way or another.

It will determine your preoccupations

The things you devote your time to, and on which your mind dwells, are your preoccupations. A person's preoccupation comes from the person's sense of priorities. Instead of spending and devoting time to trivialities, the person with eternity in view devotes and spends time on the things which will matter before the King on His return. Nothing pleases a master like returning to find the servants doing the things he expects them to do. Do you recall the parable of the unmerciful servant? He preoccupied himself with things he wasn't asked to do. He was asked to give his fellow servants their food at the appointed time but because he did not have his master's return in view he spent his time disciplining his fellow servants. Of course when his mastered returned, I need not tell you it was trouble for him.

It will determine your pursuits

Your pursuits are your short and long term goals, determined by your priorities and preoccupations. What are your long and short term goals? If you are living with eternity in view they should be things which matter to the heartbeat of God; things in accordance with God's will for your life. I want you to take a moment and look at your pursuits! What do they tell you? Are they in line with what heaven expects of you? Are they in accordance with the will of God for your life? Because heaven's perspective is all that matters to you, the only thing that counts should be what pleases the Father's heart; that which resonates with His heartbeat.

It will determine your purity

There are many who call upon His Holy Name but who do not keep their lives pure. The simple reason is that they have relegated the promise of His coming to the background. Because the coming of the Lord is not eminent to such, they can afford to contaminate themselves with whatever they can lay their hands and eyes on. The Bible says those who hope in the coming of the Lord purify themselves. This purification is of the spirit, soul, and body. When you see the coming of the Lord as a matter of urgency, you will not live with any sin in your life even for one minute. Those who expect His coming also know that nothing impure will be taken along, so they cleanse themselves by the blood, and align their actions and priorities in the direction of holiness.

It will determine your purpose

Your purpose is the overriding goal of your life; all other goals are a derivative of your purpose. And your purpose is a culmination of your platform, perspective, priorities, preoccupations, pursuits, and purity.

Chapter Reflection

The urgency with which you live pivots on your expectation of the return of the King. Those who want to maximize this last hour must be those doing all in preparation for the soon coming King. What are your priorities? How are they tied to the coming Kingdom of God and His Christ? What principles guide your life's choices? Ask the Lord to fill your heart with a longing expectation for His coming.

Chapter Nine

Faith in God's Promises

For your life to count for time and for eternity, you must be one who acts on the promises of the Lord in His word and to you as an individual. People make the difference based on how they believe the word of God for themselves. God has given His word to each one of us but it is our responsibility to appropriate and act on it. The spiritual and physical differences between your today and tomorrow will depend greatly on your attitude to the promises of God as revealed in His word. The truth is God does make promises to us as individuals as we come into His presence in worship and adoration. For most people these promises and words to us end in the place of worship when the excitement is over. The word of God must be received, believed, meditated on, and acted on for it to bring forth the fruit for which it was released.

Simeon believed the promise of God to him that he was not going to die until he had seen the Lord's Christ.

What kept him living in expectation for the consolation of Israel was the promise of God to him. Sometimes what will keep you in the face of adversity and make your life count for time and for eternity is the word of the Lord to you. God's promise is what will give you hope in a hopeless situation. It is what will make you laugh in the midst of painful circumstances and provide you a lifeline when others have concluded that you are going to give up. While his contemporaries were dying, he lived because he had the promise of God upon his life. While people thought he ought to have died, he kept living because the word of God to him was sustaining him.

God's promise to you will sustain and preserve you in difficult times. His promise to you is the seed for your future, the anchor to your dreams, and the magnet for divine favor. Are there some promises God has made to you in your personal time of worship to Him? Are there some promises in the word you are waiting to see made manifest in your life? You can write them down and proclaim that each one of them will come to pass. Simeon, after seeing the baby Jesus, took him in his arms and said, "Sovereign Lord, as you have promised, you now…" There is one thing I want you to know: between the stating of a promise and its manifestation is a time interval within which many things happen. We will talk about this in detail later. But there is one vital factor which must sustain the promise within this time of its gestation- your faith in the promise. Faith is the womb that carries and nurtures the promise of God from its conception, through gestation, to delivery. In the next lines I want to share with you the kinds of promises which are found in the word of God.

Kinds of Promises

Conditional promises: These are promises with preconditions clearly tied to them. For such a promise to be fulfilled, all the preconditions must be fulfilled, without which the *promisee* has no right to claim the promise, for example, God's promise to His people in 2 Chronicles 7: 14. Its fulfilment depends largely on the *promisee*.

Absolute promises: These are promises with no preconditions. Such promises depend largely on their and often take the form of an oath. The *promisee* has virtually no part to play but to expect and receive the fulfilment of the promise. What counts here is the integrity of the *promisor*; as long as the he can be trusted, the *promisee* can wait with eager expectation to see the promise fulfilled. An example of such a promise is God's promise of a son to Abram.

Absolute-conditional promises: These are promises which are in two phases, one phase being conditional and the other phase being absolute. Here the *promisor* promises to do something, and after he does it, the *promisee* has to do something for the last part of the deal to be fulfilled. Such take the form of covenants. An example of such a promise is God's promise to Abram about his descendants inheriting the Land.

So, for the promise of God to you to have a lasting impact, you must understand what kind of promise it is and what role, if there is any, you have to play for its fulfillment. This is vital and pivotal on the effect of your faith to see the promise come to fulfillment. In Simeon's case, it was an absolute promise and all he had to do was to have faith in the promise and in the God who made the promise. Even if it meant that Simeon had to live for a thousand years, he would have been kept for that long for God's word to be fulfilled to him.

After understanding the kind of promise God has made in His word or to you as an individual, the next thing for you to do is to understand the time frame of the promise.

With respect to time, we can also see that sometimes God states a promise without giving any time frame (for instance the first and second time He stated His promise to Abraham in Genesis 15 and 17 respectively). However, in Genesis eighteen, by the time He was stating the promise for the third time, He gave them a time frame within which the promise would be realized, and that was within a year. These two points of knowing the nature and timeframe of the promise are important for the exercise of your faith. It is because Abraham never understood God's time frame at first that his faith wavered and waned as the years went by, thereby leading to the bringing forth of Ishmael. For your life to count for time and for eternity you must exercise faith in the promises of God in the face of uncertainty.

Like I said before, between the time when a promise is stated and the time when it is fulfilled is an interval which determines a lot. Your composure within that time interval of gestation will determine whether the promise will come to pass or will abort, depending on its kind of course. What are some things which happen within the gestation period?

The testing of the Promise

During the gestation period of God's promise in the womb of faith, the promise itself will be tested. Just like a pregnancy comes under severe tests, so the promise comes under severe tests. Many things will happen within this time frame that will make you question and ponder and wonder if you ever heard God correctly. Things will seem to go in the opposite direction to where you intend going. All you have to do is go back to the God who spoke to you, in worship, adoration, and thanksgiving. One thing I want to let you know is that God will do all to protect and to preserve His promise. Isaac, God's promise to Abraham was tested even after the promise had been realized. But God preserved and sustained him.

The testing of your faith

The testing of the promise automatically tests your faith in the One who made the promise. During difficult times, doubt will assail your mind, but by faith you have to overcome and keep out the doubts. Exercising your faith will mean you making confessions and declarations which are in line with the promise God has given you, even in the midst of contrary and controversial circumstances. It is the testing of your faith that will produce the patient endurance and perseverance you will need to carry the promise to maturity when it begins to unfold.

When all has been said and done, God's promise will come to fulfillment in God's way, at the time God has promised, no matter the circumstances.

Chapter Reflection

What are some Divine promises to you as an individual? Do you still have faith to you them fulfilled? Have you fulfilled the conditions? What about His general promises to all who call on the Name of His Son? Are you standing steadfast, believing and appropriating them for yourself, family, co-workers etc.? God is always faithful to His Word, just stand the tests and enjoy His promises.

Chapter Ten
Knowledge of the God of the Promise

I know this chapter seems out of place, for it was supposed to come first. It is coming as the last chapter to crown all we have said so far. In fact because I have written much about the knowledge of God in my other books, I was not going to include a whole chapter on it here until now that the Holy Spirit has led me to include it. When it originates from Him, it always makes the difference!

Your knowledge and faith in the God you serve will determine your composure and comportment in the controversial and contradictory circumstances of life. It will determine and guide your reaction to provocation and pressure that comes in the heat of adverse circumstances of life. It will determine the outcome of opportunities that adversity comes along with. Yes you read that correctly, I mean opportunities.

Often people concentrate on the difficulties that adversity brings and fail to step into the opportunities in the difficulties. I want you to know that there is an opportunity in every difficulty or controversy in life. You need just open your eyes, or better still ask the Lord to open your eyes, so that you can see and make use of them. Your knowledge of God will determine your travail and triumph in the test and trials that come to you.

In writing to God's people scattered all over the world, Peter said, "Grace and peace be yours in abundance through the knowledge of God and of Jesus our Lord. His divine power has given us everything we need for a godly life through our knowledge of him who called us by his own glory and goodness". (2 Peter 1:2-3)

From the above verses we can bring out the following:

The degree of grace and peace available to you in life depends on your knowledge of God: it is the availability of grace and your ability to walk in that grace that determines what you accomplish in life. You need grace to function and succeed in life and to accomplish your divine assignment, and the way to tap from that grace is through your knowledge of God. Your knowledge of God will give you access to the grace of God. It is God's grace that provides, protects, preserves, and promotes in life. You want abundant grace to be yours? Then grow in your intimate knowledge of the Lord, of His Christ, and of His Holy Spirit. Also the peace of God that you need to sail through turbulent and tumultuous circumstances is available to you through your knowledge of Him.

Sometimes things happen that will shatter your life to pieces and destroy your dreams and aspirations if the peace of God does not reign in your heart. The Bible talks of a peace that passes all understanding; this is the peace which is manifested when others think you should be raving, racing, ranting, or throwing stones and spears at everybody. It is such peace that will cause you, like David in the midst of thousands of troops seeking his life and his throne- led by his own son, to say, "I lie down and sleep; I wake again, because the LORD sustains me. I will not fear though tens of thousands assail me on every side." (Ps 3:5-6) What caused David to maintain such peaceful and serene composure when all around him was calling for worry and anxiety? It was his knowledge of the God he served. He knew that he was going to sleep and rise again; he refused to fear the tens of thousands that were drawn against him, because he knew his God.

Everything you need for life and godliness comes through your knowledge of Him: All you need to excel in this life and beyond, for your life to count beyond your lifetime, in time and eternity has been made available to you. But it is your knowledge of God that makes them available to you. That is why your knowledge of God is both the foundation and the chief cornerstone in building the house of your destiny. So instead of running after the things you figure you need for life, run after God and grow in your knowledge of Him. In this way you gain access into the divine provision for life and godliness.

To live a life that counts, you must know and believe that:

1. Jehovah sees: there are times your whole life will seem engulfed in the dark and impenetrable cloud of uncertainty and ambiguity; times when you ask yourself if anyone is seeing your predicament. Has that ever happened to you? It happened to the children of Israel in the days of their slavery to pharaoh in the land of Egypt. In the midst of all these seemingly endless trials they came to the conclusion that Jehovah was not seeing what was happening to them. That's why when Moses had his encounter with God, Jehovah introduced Himself as the God of their fathers and said, "I have indeed seen the misery of my people…" (Ex 3:7a) You will have to know and believe that Jehovah sees. He sees the big picture of your life as well as the minutest details of what happens each second of your life. Knowing that Jehovah sees will make you to

understand that He is still in charge of everything. Meditate on the following verses:

> "For the eyes of the LORD range throughout the earth to strengthen those whose hearts are fully committed to him." (2Ch 16:9a)

> "But the eyes of the LORD are on those who fear him,
>   on those whose hope is in his unfailing love" (Ps 33:18)

> "My eyes are on all their ways; they are not hidden from me, nor is their sin concealed from my eyes." (Jer 16:17)

The eyes of the Lord are ranging over the whole earth to strengthen those whose hearts are fully committed to Him. When you know this you will ensure that your whole heart is committed to the Lord. One thing that makes people ineffective in their Christian life is halfhearted commitment to the Lord. When you know that God sees and that His eyes are on those who fear Him, you will live to walk in the fear of the Lord. And the fear of the Lord is what will bring a difference in your life. You will hope in the unfailing love of God when all else around you fades and fails. Finally, when you know that Jehovah sees your ways, you will cease to live a double life. You will avoid the path of sin even when you are where no one else sees you and sin presents itself as it often does. Because you know that Jehovah sees you, you will keep away from sin. The God you serve sees!

2. Jehovah hears: knowing, believing, and understanding that Jehovah, the God you serve hears will also make you live a life that counts for time and for eternity. Again, He revealed to Moses saying, "I have heard them crying out…" (Ex 3:7b) We already talked extensively on this in an earlier

chapter, so it's needless to repeat it here. If your life must count you must know and believe that your God hears you when you call, when you cry, and when you talk.

3. Jehovah knows: for your life to count, you must know your God as the God who knows. One who knows the end from the beginning! He knows the path you should take and the difficulties which lie on that path.

- He knows the plans He has for you. When you know that God has plans for your life and that He knows those plans, you will live knowing there is a destiny you must fulfill, and that nothing happens to you by chance. You will seek to align your actions with God's plans for a life. (see Jer 29:11)
- He knows your thoughts. Knowing that God knows your thoughts makes you conscious and selective about the thoughts you allow

in your mind. You will want to think in line with His word and nature. (see Ps 94:11)

- He knows how to rescue: have you ever found yourself in a situation where you wonder how you will ever come out? It happens sometimes! But you must come to the place where you know that your God has not lost options on how to rescue you from any situation in which you may find yourself. When you know and believe this, then deliverance will always come to you even when you think the situation is hopeless. (see 2Pe 2:9)

- He knows those who are His: many people think they can play games with God. And by so doing they are wasting their time and resources; of course they are not living a life that counts, not in this life, not in eternity. Do not waste time playing the game of religion. All who engage in this game come out as losers. The Bible says God knows those who are His. And that everyone who is His departs from iniquity. In simple terms they have taken a conscious decision to abandon sin in all its forms and manifestations. (see2Ti 2:19)

4. Jehovah is concerned: there are people who see your predicament, they hear you crying and groaning, they know what has to be done, but show no concern. Your God is not like that. He sees, hears, knows, and is concerned about you. He told Moses, "…and I am concerned about their suffering." God is concerned about all that concerns you as a unique individual. He wants the best for you and is working to bring that best to fulfillment. He is concerned about your health, about your

finances, about your relationships, about your job, about your present and your future. God is concerned about all that concerns you!

5. Jehovah is able: some people see, hear, know, are concerned, but are not able to do anything about your situation. In many cases that is the bitter truth and many of God's children think God is not able to do a thing about the circumstances surrounding them. Like the man whose son was possessed by the spirits that wanted to kill him, some are saying to the Lord, "if you can do anything…" For your life to count you must come to the place where you know your God as one with whom all things are possible, with Him nothing is impossible. The God you serve is more than able to:

- Make all grace abound towards you (2Co 9:8): we said earlier that grace is what you need to excel in all you do, and God is able to make all grace abound towards you. The grace to love all men, the grace to forgive, the grace to be victorious, the grace to make the right choices, the grace to endure difficult moments, the grace to prosper, and the grace to walk in holiness and purity. God is able to make all this abound in you.

- Do exceedingly more than you ask or imagine (Eph 3:20): if your life must count, you must ask and trust God for ridiculously big things. No matter how big your request is, God is able to do exceedingly abundantly more than what you have asked. God is more than able to do things in you and through you that will make men and women marvel at His goodness and greatness.

- Save to the uttermost (He 7:25): salvation is a total package for the total man, and God is able to save completely from any and every unpleasant situation.
- Keep you from falling (Jude 24): many believers are too afraid to fall that they fail to do anything for the kingdom. They try and labor to keep themselves from falling and therefore live ineffective lives. Listen, God has promised to keep you from falling and is well able to do so. All you have to do is heed the warnings in the Bible and follow the leading of the Holy Spirit. Do not be afraid little flock, He who watches over you will never sleep or slumber and will keep you from falling and

present you to Himself. Paul said he knew whom he had believed in and was persuaded that He is able to keep and to guide that which has been entrusted to Him. All you need is to entrust yourself to His care and live your life one day at a time.

- Deliver you(Da 3:17): Daniel and his contemporaries, Mishael, Hannaniah, and Azariah, made their life to count in their lifetime and beyond because they understood that the God they served was able to deliver them from any and every situation. As a result they refused to compromise in idolatry and were willing to lay down their lives. Of course the Lord did not fail them. He showed up on their behalf to prove them true. The

God they served was able to deliver them from the fiery furnace. This calls for reckless abandonment in His hands.

- Establish you (Ro 16:25): the God you serve is able to establish you in the ministry, business, profession or whatever He has called you to do. He is able to establish you in the faith and to establish the work of your hands and make it prosper. Our God is the God who establishes. When you know and believe this, you are able to move out in faith to do what He has laid on your heart to do for the Kingdom.

- Help you (He 2:18): do you need help in any area of your life? Of course you surely do every second of your life, and His help is readily available to you each time you acknowledge the fact that you need it. There is enormous divine help available to you in every area of your life. The God you serve is a God who is able to help you. The Bible says you should approach the throne of grace to find grace and mercy to help you in times of need. Make the difference by using the help that is available to you from above. Mordecai told Esther that if she was not going to help the Jews in their situation , help was going to come from somewhere else. This is because he understood that Jehovah is able to help in any and every situation. Fix your eyes on Him and on nothing else. The Psalmist said, "I lift up my eyes to the mountains—where does my help come from? ² My help comes from the LORD, the Maker of heaven and earth." (Ps 121:1-2) Open the scroll (Rev 5:5): the secret to your future and destiny is wrapped in God's scroll and there is just one person worthy to take that scroll and to open it. Because of this He is able to reveal to you portions of your future and destiny, downloading them to your spirit man. He is the revealer of mysteries and He is able to make them known to you.

6. Jehovah is willing: many people do not doubt God's ability to do anything; their doubt comes when they are questioned about God's willingness. They are

not very sure whether He is willing to do it for them. The God you serve is not a reluctant God; He is more than willing to do all what He is able to do. He is willing to make all grace abound towards you; willing to do exceedingly abundantly more than you can ever ask or think; willing to save to the uttermost; willing to deliver; willing to keep you from falling; willing to help you; willing to establish you willing to open the scroll for you to take a look into it with the eyes of your spirit. You remember the leper who came to Him and said. "Lord if you are willing…." (Mt 8:1-3) And the Lord said to him, "I am willing…" O! That you will know and be sure that God is willing. He is not reluctant but is willing to heal you, to bless you again and again and again. He is willing to sustain and to preserve you. He is willing to promote you and raise you above your contemporaries. Your God is willing!

7. Jehovah is sovereign: sometimes you will find yourself in circumstances for which no reasonable explanation can be given. You may even seek spiritual answers and not find any in such moments. The enemy may mock at you and taunt you for believing in the Lord and ask you provocative questions. When such moments arrive there is one thing I want you to know; it's not everything you'll find an explanation for. I know there are people willing and "able" to provide explanations and give you "valid" reasons why some things happen the way they happen. Well, I am not one of such. I believe there are things we will never be able to understand on this side of eternity. Read the following verse and see that there are situations in which the enemy will seize the opportunity to mock:

"My bones suffer mortal agony as my foes taunt me, saying to me all day long, "Where is your God?" (Ps 42:10)

"Why should the nations say,
"Where is their God?" Before our eyes,
make known among the nations that you avenge the outpoured blood
of your servants." (Ps 79:10)

"My tears have been my food day and night, while people say to me all day long,
"Where is your God?" (Ps 42:3)

In such situations you may have no other response but to say, "Why do the nations say, "Where is their God?" Our God is in heaven; he does whatever pleases him."

You are serving a God who is sovereign and does whatever pleases Him. David's understanding of this made him refuse to fight unnecessary battles. He saw everything as coming from the sovereign hand of God. I personally don't believe in chance. I believe everything is divinely planed or orchestrated, or to the least permitted by Him. Let me end this chapter by leaving you with an entire psalm to meditate on, Psalm 135:

Praise the LORD.[a]

Praise the name of the LORD;
praise him, you servants of the LORD,
² you who minister in the house of the LORD,
in the courts of the house of our God.

³ Praise the LORD, for the LORD is good;
sing praise to his name, for that is pleasant.
⁴ For the LORD has chosen Jacob to be his own,
Israel to be his treasured possession.

⁵ I know that the LORD is great,
   that our Lord is greater than all gods.
⁶ The LORD does whatever pleases him,
   in the heavens and on the earth,
   in the seas and all their depths.
⁷ He makes clouds rise from the ends of the earth;
   he sends lightning with the rain
   and brings out the wind from his storehouses.

⁸ He struck down the firstborn of Egypt,
   the firstborn of people and animals.
⁹ He sent his signs and wonders into your midst, Egypt,
   against Pharaoh and all his servants.
¹⁰ He struck down many nations
   and killed mighty kings—
¹¹ Sihon king of the Amorites,

Og king of Bashan,
and all the kings of Canaan—
¹² and he gave their land as an inheritance,
an inheritance to his people Israel.

¹³ Your name, LORD, endures forever,
your renown, LORD, through all generations.
¹⁴ For the LORD will vindicate his people
and have compassion on his servants.

¹⁵ The idols of the nations are silver and gold,
made by human hands.
¹⁶ They have mouths, but cannot speak,
eyes, but cannot see.
¹⁷ They have ears, but cannot hear,
nor is there breath in their mouths.
¹⁸ Those who make them will be like them,
and so will all who trust in them.

[19] All you Israelites, praise the LORD;
   house of Aaron, praise the LORD;
[20] house of Levi, praise the LORD;
   you who fear him, praise the LORD.
[21] Praise be to the LORD from Zion,
   to him who dwells in Jerusalem.

   Praise the LORD.

In Conclusion

We have looked in detail at ten ways in which you can make your life to count for time and for eternity. Now the ball is in your court. It is high time you stopped living a trivial life and become a man or woman of consequence. Become a man or woman of background exploits, one who knows Jehovah as the God who hears. Live in righteousness, be wholeheartedly devoted to the Lord, and seek to live a life filled with the Holy Spirit. Let your life be marked by the anointing of the Holy Spirit. Live a life that is marked by the leadership of the Holy Spirit. Live in expectation of the return of Christ Jesus. Have faith in God's promises, and know the God you serve. In this way you will make your life to count for time and for eternity.

If you have been blessed by what we have shared hear, we will like to hear from you and offer you help in your walk as you seek to make your life count.

www.ingramcontent.com/pod-product-compliance
Lightning Source LLC
Chambersburg PA
CBHW020658300426
44112CB00007B/434